Thursday's Ladie

A play by
Loleh Bellon

Translated by
Barbara Bray

Samuel French – London
New York – Sydney – Toronto – Hollywood

CAST

Sonia, in her sixties
Victor, her son: 40
Marie, in her sixties
Hélène, in her sixties
Jean, Hélène's brother, Marie's husband. He is as old as they remember him
The Voice of Sonia's Mother

The age of the three women varies: sometimes we see them at their present age, sometimes as eight years old, sometimes as fifty, and so on. The same with Victor.

But these changes, instead of being shown by such artifices as changes of costume or make-up, or signalled by music or lighting effects, are indicated simply through the characters' different ways of moving and feeling at the different stages in their lives. This effect is difficult to achieve but essential to the play.

AUTHOR'S NOTE

Thursday used to be a school holiday in France. Now it is Wednesday, and modern schoolgirls may eventually be "Wednesday's Ladies".

THURSDAY'S LADIES

Presented by Toby Rowland and Robert Burns, by arrangement with Louis Benjamin for Stoll Moss Theatres Ltd, at the Apollo Theatre, London, on 9th September, 1987, with the following cast of characters:

Sonia	Dorothy Tutin
Marie	Eileen Atkins
Hélène	Siân Phillips
Victor	Albert Welling
Jean	Jeremy Brudenell

Directed by Frank Hauser
Designed by Peter Rice

The action of the play is set in Sonia's apartment in Paris—winter, 1975

THURSDAY'S LADIES

Sonia's Apartment in Paris. Winter, 1975

When the CURTAIN *rises, Sonia is lying on the divan upstage with her back to the audience. She is wearing a loose house frock or overall*

The doorbell rings. Pause. There is the sound of a key in the lock

Victor, Sonia's forty-year-old son, enters. He looks round, sees Sonia, and tiptoes over to her

Victor (*suddenly*) Oo-oo!
Sonia Vishya! How did you get in?
Victor Down the chimney. (*He laughs*) Guess what I found under the mat?
Sonia (*shrugging*) That was for Marie and Hélène.
Victor Oh yes, I forgot—it's Thursday. (*He goes over and kisses her*) Right—well, I'll leave you now, Mamotchka, and come back later.
Sonia (*getting up*) No—stay for a bit. They never come before four.
Victor Of course. The famous tea!

Pause. Victor roams around the room like someone quite at home. He opens a cupboard and helps himself to a biscuit. Sonia watches him

Sonia I waited for you on Sunday.
Victor Sunday?
Sonia You were coming to dinner, remember? I made stuffed cabbage and chocolate pudding. I've been finishing them up all week.
Victor Isn't there anything to drink in this place?
Sonia You drink too much.
Victor Just because you have gallstones doesn't mean I have a weak liver!
Sonia Three Sundays and three let-downs! That's the last time I ask you to dinner!
Victor Wait till I tell you what happened! The phone rang at seven in the morning. It was Pierre. My friend with the garage.

Sonia says nothing. She gets a bottle and a glass out of the cupboard

Guess what he'd found by the side of the road? (*Pause*) A six-cylinder nineteen twenty-two Hamilcar!

Sonia (*looking at his jacket*) You've lost a button.
Victor It's in my pocket.
Sonia Give it here.

Victor takes off his jacket and hands it over

Victor The marvellous little C Six—the one with two overhead camshafts and a Rootes compressor ...
Sonia Haven't you already got a Hamilcar?
Victor Mine's only got four cylinders. And I'm still working on it.
Sonia (*going to look for her work-basket in the closet*) But it *is* a Hamilcar!
Victor Yes ... The model with the narrow mudguards and unaligned seats ... You bought me one once in the bazaar in the rue de Nesles. For my birthday. It was red. With pedals.
Sonia And what happened to it?
Victor You gave it to the concierge's little boy while I was away at summer camp.
Sonia (*coming back*) Not that one—the other one!
Victor Mine?
Sonia No, the one on Sunday!
Victor Who knows? It's got an English number plate.
Sonia What about the driver?
Victor In hospital. (*Pause*) But the Hamilcar's a wreck! I didn't touch it. Just put a bit of plastic over it to keep the weather out. The rust gets to everything at this time of year.
Sonia (*sitting down and starting to sew*) Was he all on his own?
Victor We saw a couple of Englishmen lurking round the remains ...
Sonia Relatives of his?
Victor They'd brought a trailer to take it back to England. They told us the chap who owns it found it buried away in a stable in the Vaucluse ... Three years he'd spent rebuilding that car. He'd only just started to drive it. What rotten luck! If only I could afford the engine—(*taking a package out of his pocket*) I found this lying in the grass.
Sonia What is it?
Victor Open it and see.

She undoes the package

Sonia The radiator cap! (*She shines it on her dress*) It's very pretty.
Victor Do you like it?
Sonia Yes.
Victor (*in a lordly manner*) Keep it, then.
Sonia (*kissing him*) Thank you.
Victor As soon as I manage to get one on the road I'll take you on the Paris-Nice rally, or the vintage car race in Provence ... By the way, Mamotchka, could you oblige me with a bit of the ready? I'll let you have it back of course. My photographs will be out next week. The paper's had them a month.
Sonia How much?

Victor Five hundred francs . . . Four . . . Whatever you can manage.

Sonia What is it today—the twenty-third? If you could wait till tomorrow— I'd rather see what's in my account before I write a cheque.

Victor What happened to your lump sum? All gone?

Sonia What happened to the Hamilcar shed, pray? How did we pay for that?

Victor Its little nest!

Sonia You said it'd be a good investment, what with devaluation and so on . . . But if I were to be ill now . . .

Victor Don't be morbid! You're as fit as a fiddle!

Sonia touches wood

What time shall I come then?

Sonia Come for lunch. I'll go and get the money out of the bank in the morning. That'll save you a journey.

Victor Right. Now I must rush. Pierre saw an advert that looked interesting. Some Hartford shock absorbers. (*He fiddles with the lamp on her desk*) Can I borrow a bulb? My last one went phut this morning.

Sonia Don't take that one! How am I supposed to read this evening?

Victor Use braille! (*He kisses her*) All right, keep your old lights! (*He goes out, then pokes his head back in again*) Ciao!

Victor disappears

Sonia goes to and fro, putting away the bottle and glass, talking to herself

Sonia He's too nice . . . Always running round after those spare parts . . . Well, every man to his taste. What can I give him for lunch . . . ? I'll have to go out anyway—there's nothing in the fridge. (*Pause. She picks up a kimono from a chair and puts it on over her dress during the following*) I didn't realize there was more than one kind of Hamilcar . . . Complicated things, cars. (*She looks at herself in the mirror*) I look like a lampshade . . . ! Perhaps with a belt . . . (*Pause*) I wonder how much I've got left in the bank . . . ? Can't be much . . . About a couple of thousand francs . . . (*She gives a little laugh*) The little red pedal car—in nineteen forty he wanted to pedal off in it with all the refugees . . . Furious, he was! (*Pause*) Did he give me back the two hundred I lent him last month? I can't remember.

There is a ring at the door

(*Going to answer it*) Coming! Coming!

Sonia exits

Marie (*off*) Isn't it cold? Either I was dreaming or I passed Victor just now in the street . . . Am I the first?

Sonia (*off*) He just dropped in to say hallo.

Marie (*off*) So! He's alive! Are you all right now?

Sonia (*off*) Oh yes . . .

Marie (*off*) I hope he apologized?

Sonia (*off*) Of course. He had some important business out of town.

Marie enters, without her coat

Marie In that case! (*She notices the kimono*) Where did you get that marvellous kimono?

Sonia It was my grandmother Suliakov's dressing-gown. (*She puts on a Russian accent*) "Real kimono. Hand made. Such a beauty!"

Marie (*stroking the material*) I remembered it as pink satin, with gold birds on it . . . The "beauty" 's a bit faded. Have you noticed the lining?

Sonia It hasn't been out of the drawer for twenty years.

Marie Gold thread . . . Chinese silk . . . the treasures of Marco Polo . . .

Sonia I've been trailing round the shops since the crack of dawn—I'm exhausted.

Marie (*turning over the parcels on the table*) What utterly useless objects have you been buying now?

Sonia Didn't I tell you? Some friends of Hélène's have asked me to a party on New Year's Eve. Fancy dress. I don't know that it'll be all that amusing. But anyway not so dreary as seeing the New Year in on my own watching the telly.

Marie I didn't know people still gave fancy-dress parties.

Sonia (*showing off her kimono*) Madam Butterfly. Do you think it's a good idea?

Marie (*laughing*) Brings out your oriental streak—cruel and mysterious!

Sonia I've got all this stuff, but I'll never be able to make myself up like a Japanese!

Marie It's not difficult. A couple of strokes at the corner of your eyes to make them look slanting. Have you got an eyebrow pencil? Sit down. (*She picks a pencil up from the table and starts to make Sonia up*) Like this . . . There . . . You see?

Sonia looks at herself in the glass

Sonia It cuts right across the wrinkles. I look awful.

Marie No you don't, you look very nice—no-one's going to look at you through a microscope! And then you slope your eyebrows upwards . . . Oh, you've got a few grey ones!

Sonia Not enough to make it worth having them dyed!

Marie (*stepping back to see the effect*) It'd look even better with false eyelashes.

Sonia I'd never manage to stick them on!

Marie Wait, I haven't finished. (*She outlines Sonia's mouth*) A little cupid's bow . . . There! Have you got any light powder?

Sonia points to a compact on the table

Skin like a peach . . .

Sonia shuts her eyes as Marie applies the powder puff

Sonia (*smiling*) More like an old prune . . . ! Won't I be a sensation! I've even bought a wig. (*She takes one out of a box*) I had no choice, with my hair. (*She puts on the wig. She coughs*)

Marie (*passing her the hairpins*) Have you got a cough?

Sonia I've had it since Sunday. I went and saw Kahn, and it seems there's nothing the matter with me—it's just nervous.

Marie You're rather curly for a Japanese!

Sonia (*fixing a flower on either side of the wig*) What do you think? Cheers it up, doesn't it?

Marie One's enough. You don't want to overdo it. (*She removes one of the flowers*) The sky's always grey now in Tokyo. Everyone's eyes hurt because of the smog. And there are no more swallows ...

Sonia isn't listening; she's rehearsing her entrance, humming a tune and mincing along in time to it

Sonia (*giving an oriental bow*) I'm sure to trip over my kimono with all those people watching! Wouldn't you like to come with me?

Marie Very kind of you, but no thanks.

A ring at the bell

Sonia (*indicating her costume and wig*) Here comes my first audience!

Sonia goes to open the door

Hélène (*off*) What on earth are you got up like that for?

Sonia (*off*) Marie and I are trying out my make-up for New Year's Eve ...

Hélène enters wearing her outdoor coat and carrying a package. Sonia follows

Hélène You look like a madam in a Shanghai brothel. (*To Marie*) You don't look up to much either. (*To Sonia*) I found the blend you were looking for, Sonitchka. (*She holds out the package*)

Sonia (*taking it*) Oh, terrific—I'll put some in the teapot.

Marie I'm not sleeping very well at the moment. I must phone Mercier and get him to renew my prescription.

Sonia goes out with her party things and Hélène's coat

Hélène (*to Marie*) I've been telling you for thirty years you shouldn't take those barbiturates. You think too much. You make a mountain out of everything. (*Pause*) How are the girls?

Marie Very well. I had lunch at Laura's yesterday and she asked me to give her auntie a kiss.

They kiss

There!

Hélène Is her work going well?

Marie Up and down. There's not much building going on at the moment ... It's a thin time for architects.

Hélène How about Jeanne?

Marie I had a line from her this morning. She's bringing the little girls to Paris for Christmas. I'm thrilled to bits ...

Hélène (*looking in her compact mirror and repairing her lipstick*) My charming nieces don't do much to cultivate their expectations.

Marie (*finishing clearing the table*) You could see them more often if you
wanted to. It's up to you!

Hélène (*shutting her compact*) When is your family going to produce some
men? All these women—you can't breathe for them!

Marie Your brother had nothing to do with it, I suppose?

Hélène Your mother, your aunt, you, your daughters, your granddaughters
. . . Nothing but women, always women!

Marie Why haven't *you* ever tried?

Hélène I don't like children.

Pause

Marie That's a nice jumper. Cashmere?

Hélène I got it in a sale. (*She looks round the room*) Squalid as ever. How
can she live in such a place?

Marie I like these old apartments where everything's a bit crooked—where
you're always knocking into things!

Hélène Don't be silly! If it was completely done up . . . But it's dirty and
dark and inconvenient—I couldn't stick it for three days!

Marie She's not likely to go spending money on it now she's sold it for an
annuity.

Hélène She might live another thirty years!

Marie Anyhow, she's already spent her bonus.

Hélène Bonus?

Marie Yes, the lump sum. She gets twelve hundred francs a month from the
annuity, but she got a down payment when she signed the contract.

Hélène That was the forty thousand francs she came into in June?

Marie Yes.

Hélène And she's spent the lot.

Marie Apparently.

They start to lay the table for tea, starting with the cloth

This is a pretty cloth—where's it from?

Hélène Russia, I should imagine. The cousin in Vladivostock . . .

Marie (*smoothing the cloth*) Very pretty.

Hélène I went to see Tavel on Tuesday. He wanted me to sign some papers
about the apartment in Nice. (*Pause*) He ought to be giving Sonia a ring.
Her shares are going up.

Marie Has she got any left?

Hélène From her grandfather Suliakov. The one who owned some ships in
the Baltic and left all his money to the Academy of Sciences . . . But he did
leave her a few shares! They weren't worth the paper they were written on
. . . they just lay mouldering in some drawer . . . and now they've suddenly
come to life again.

Marie After twenty years?

*They get cups and saucers and small plates out of the cupboard. Every
Thursday they go through the same routines. Laying the table for tea is a sort
of ritual. They are setting the scene for their memories*

Hélène Some business of striking oil in the North Sea—I didn't quite get the ins and outs ... Anyway, it should be worth about fifty thousand francs.
Marie How wonderful! There *is* something to be said for capitalism! ... She'll be able to have the place redecorated—you'll like that.
Hélène Don't worry—Victor will grab the lot.

Sonia enters wearing a proper dress and without the wig

Sonia (*removing the make-up*) What will my Victor grab?
Hélène Some nineteen twenty-five hooters I saw in the flea-market.
Sonia Oh, he *will* be pleased!
Hélène You haven't got two cups that match ... and there are ten saucers to every cup ...
Sonia Guess what my Victor found, in a ditch near Arpajon? A little C Six ...
Marie What's that?
Sonia (*with a superior air*) A Hamilcar ...
Hélène He didn't find a job too, by any chance?
Sonia Oh, he does so many things already! An art magazine has commissioned him to do some photographs for a special number on model cars. Haven't I ever shown you his photos? They're marvellous! He's got real talent!

Sonia disappears

The other two get some cutlery out of the cupboard. Pause

Marie (*smiling*) Will he really grab her money, do you think?
Hélène She can hardly keep body and soul together just with the annuity and the miserable amount she earns. Now she might be able to see her way clear for a bit, it'd be too bad if he went and filched it all!
Marie But what if it makes her happy? What if she wants to spend all her money on a gigolo? It so happens the gigolo is her son, who really loves her. She's lucky, really.
Hélène She's spoiled him, indulged his every whim! He'll never cut himself loose from her apron-strings ...
Marie Not if she can help it.

They arrange table-napkins, sugar-bowl and sugar-tongs on the table. Pause

Hélène I met Paul Fabre last week. He's got terribly old—I scarcely recognized him. He looks appalling.
Marie Paul Fabre ... Jean's friend? I haven't seen him for at least fifteen years. (*Pause*) No—not since Jean's funeral.
Hélène Why do you always call him Jean? It does irritate me. We always called him Jeannot at home.
Marie Yes, but he preferred to be called Jean.

Pause

Hélène Fabre told me there was talk of a new edition of their paper on the corpuscular effects of light.
Marie Really?

Hélène Hadn't you heard?

Marie No ... I've been sent one or two articles lately about his work ...

Pause. They put a tea-cosy and a mat on the table and arrange the three chairs in front of the three cups

Hélène You never took much interest in his research, did you?

Marie How could I? Do *you* know anything about wave mathematics? No? Well then ...

Hélène Didn't that bother him sometimes?

Marie Don't make me laugh ... There can only be about thirty people in the whole world who understand what it's all about ... And you expect me ... ? And anyway, at home he couldn't even add up. He was very good at amusing the children though ...

> In the rue du Four, in times of old
> Lived father, mother, two girls and a cat.
> Jeanne was always timid, Laura was bold,
> Marie said yes, and Jean "Why not?"
> The cat said: "Miaow!"

They laugh

Sonia comes in with tea

Hélène Before you two married he used to spend whole nights arguing with Father. Mother and I used to listen openmouthed. Not understanding a word. Enchanted ... Our men!

Pause

Sonia How old would he have been now?

They sit down at the table with Sonia in the middle, Hélène on her right and Marie on her left

Marie Jean? He was seven years older than me. So he'd have been sixty-seven now.

Hélène (*to Sonia*) Can't you ever remember?

Sonia No. For me he's the eternal student.

Hélène For me he's always Jeannot.

Marie For me he's always Jean.

A young man enters upstage, dressed in the style of the nineteen thirties

Hélène (*softly*) Jeannot ...

Marie (*softly*) Jean ...

Sonia (*softly*) The eternal student ...

Jean Hallo, girls!

The three women turn round. Their manner changes immediately—the way they move, the way they speak, the language they use. They are fifteen years old

Marie Jean!

Hélène (*running over to him*) Jeannot!
Sonia What are *you* doing here?

They crowd around him, kissing him

Hélène I was just thinking about you.
Sonia Where have you sprung from?
Hélène When did you arrive?
Jean Just now. Twenty-eight hours to get back here from the Rhineland—
think of that!
Marie Are you staying long?
Hélène Oh Jeannot, I've missed you terribly!

Hélène pulls him over to the armchair and sits on his knee

Sonia What have you done with your uniform?
Jean It's in the cupboard with the moths. No more uniform. No more
square bashing. No more army of occupation. Perhaps you'd have liked
me to wear my medals?
Hélène My darling Jeannot, my buzzie . . .
Sonia (*admiringly*) Have you got some medals? (*She comes and squats by the
armchair*)

Marie remains standing where she is

Jean Oh yes. Putty ones! My dear young ladies. It's so good to see you.
Hélène My poor little buzzie, he must have been lonely, all on his own!
Jean He's grown up, your little buzzie, he's got older . . . (*To Marie*) And
you, my dear, you promised to write to me and I haven't had a line!
Marie I've been busy.
Hélène I've thought of you every day, every hour!
Jean Yes, but you're my sister—that's natural.
Hélène (*throwing her arms around him*) Your Siamese twin! I adore you!
(*She strokes the skin on his hands*) He's got such soft skin, my buzzie! But
why didn't you write to me for my birthday? I waited all day. But nothing.
I was so sad I didn't even feel like having a bath or putting on a record!
Jean (*kissing her*) You mustn't be cross with me, kid—it wasn't easy . . . (*He
leans back, stretches*) Oh, the smell of tar again at last, the petrol fumes,
the grey sky—the big city! I shan't move, I'll just bury myself at home
until the exams are over. And you girls can all make a fuss of me. (*He gets
up, goes over to Marie, and puts his hands on her shoulders*) As skinny as
ever! There are girls like that there. Standing in queues outside the baker's
shops. Dark ones with the bodies of children and a swarm of brothers and
sisters.
Hélène (*interrupting*) I thought German girls all had blue eyes and flaxen
plaits?
Jean That just shows you don't read the right books.
Sonia (*doing a few steps of the Charleston*) Hey, Jeannot, can you do this
one? It's not difficult—look!
Jean (*laughing*) You're behind the times, my girls. The Charleston's got
whiskers on!
Sonia (*stopping dancing, abashed*) Yes, but before you used to say I was too

small ... What about this one—do you know it? It's a scream! (*She starts to dance a one-step*) Come on, I'll teach you.

Jean All right.

Jean dances with Sonia. Her attitude towards him is flirtatious. Hélène and Marie just stand and watch

You've got thin.

Sonia (*proudly*) I've lost seven kilos ... That's better, isn't it?

Jean (*kissing her; touched*) Seven kilos less of Sonia!

They go on dancing

Is this right?

Sonia Very good! Did you go out much in the Rhineland?

Jean (*stopping dancing*) No.

Sonia Why?

Jean We're not very popular in that part of the world. Especially when we're in uniform.

Sonia But you looked so handsome in uniform! Like Douglas Fairbanks ...

Jean (*going and sitting down*) They don't like being reminded that they lost the war. They're cold and hungry and they've got three and a half million unemployed. I've seen middle-class men wearing hats and black ties sitting on the steps outside the soup kitchens and eating straight out of tins. I've seen girls younger than all of you prostituting themselves for a meal. Boys too. (*Pause*) But there must be some people there that dance. Just like everywhere else. Always the same ones.

Pause

Marie (*in a small voice*) Have you finished your military service?

Jean Yes. (*He gets up*) Well, my respectable young ladies, I must bid you a respectful farewell. I have a few things to do.

Sonia (*clinging to him*) Oh, do stay!

Hélène You will be home for dinner? You're not going out? Promise!

Jean Cross my heart and hope to die. And if any of you need some help with your maths I'm at your disposal.

Sonia I'm absolutely hopeless! I'm sure to have to stay down.

Jean (*to Marie*) And how's *your* work going?

Marie Fair to middling.

Sonia More middling than fair.

Marie I don't like any of the girls in my class. They're all cats.

Hélène I get on very well with *her*. We only quarrel once a day.

Jean Congratulations! (*To Marie*) Have you decided what you want to do when you leave school?

Marie Medicine.

Jean Phew! You've got some pluck ...

Hélène I went and strewed flowers on Alfred de Musset's grave on the seventy-third anniversary of his death ...

Jean He must have been pleased! Well, girls, I'll leave you to get on with your work. Cheerio!

Jean leaves

Sonia goes and preens herself in the glass, humming a tune

 Hélène (*pulling Sonia's hair*) When are you going to turn off the charm, you little horror?

Sonia Ow!!

Hélène You never stopped giving him the glad eye!

Marie Of course you can slay them all, my dear, if you try that hard.

Sonia (*plaintively*) But he *asked* me to show him——

Hélène }
Marie } (*together*) Liar!

Hélène Making googoo eyes and fluttering your eyelashes!

Sonia I don't do it on purpose ...

Hélène You really are exasperating, the way you act with men ...

Marie Anyone could do it ... Men are so stupid ... They let themselves be taken in by your tricks ...

Hélène Simpering and smirking! It's grotesque!

Sonia I can't help it—I'm made like that!

Hélène Don't think I didn't see what you're up to! Every time you move you flounce up your skirt (*she does an imitation*) so he can admire your thighs ...

Marie Your big fat thighs!

Sonia (*going back to the table, snivelling*) I'm fed up, fed up—they're both against me ... (*She sits down*)

Marie If only you carried the thing to its logical conclusion!

Hélène But no! First you lead them on, and then you leave them flat!

Marie Which is even more disgusting!

Hélène and Marie come back to the table, imitating Sonia doing the one-step

Hélène (*aping Sonia*) Can you dance this one, Jeannot?

Marie (*the same*) You looked so handsome in uniform ... Like Douglas Fairbanks ...

Hélène Do stay!

Marie Look!

They both flounce up their skirts as they sit down. Pause. All three are now sitting round the table again. Sonia pours out the tea. We are back in the present

Sonia (*sighing*) Men always thought I was no better than I should be. Perhaps it was because I had red hair ...

Hélène Henna!

Marie and Hélène laugh

Marie They thought you were no better than you should be because you did all you could to lead them on! You were never satisfied unless you had half a dozen of them trailing behind you with their tongues hanging out ...

Hélène And for what? To end up thrashing about on a mattress. Up, down, up, down. Monotonous, I call it.

Marie and Hélène laugh

Sonia (*getting up*) I've made a tart. It's sure to be awful, but you'll eat it.

Sonia goes out

Pause

Hélène I went to the cemetery on Monday.
Marie Oh yes?
Hélène I tidied up a bit. (*Pause*) And I ordered a couple of dozen lobelia plants. What do you think?
Marie Me? I don't think anything.
Hélène Your husband *is* buried there.
Marie Do you know what's left of a man after he's been dead fifteen years? Bones, teeth and hair. That's all.
Hélène If *I* neglected *my* family vault I'd feel I was letting them down. (*Pause*) How can you be so indifferent?
Marie Indifferent to what? We're not going to start that all over again, are we? My memories of Jean are inside my head. I don't have to do any gardening to revive them! (*Pause*) A stone with a name on. (*Pause*) It's different for you. You've made it your second home . . .

Pause

Hélène So what do you intend to do about the place?
Marie Place?
Hélène We discussed it last week. The vault. There's only one place left.
Marie So?
Hélène My parents bought the concession before the war. Of course, as my brother's wife you have certain rights . . .
Marie I wouldn't want to butt in!
Hélène But I've got rights too! I'm the only member of the family left . . .
Marie That's imperialism! What about Jeanne and Laura? Their name's Rouvet too, you know!
Hélène Their lives will take them elsewhere.
Marie That won't stop them dying!
Hélène Yes, but as members of other families! I want to die in *my* family. I want to be buried with them. Among them.
Marie So what do you want me to do? Go and be buried somewhere else?
Hélène We'll have to talk about it. We'll have to see.
Marie That won't make the hole any bigger.
Hélène How can you say such things? It's disgusting!
Marie It's you that's indecent! You'd like to do me out of that place, wouldn't you? The thought of me mouldering away beside your precious Jeannot keeps you awake at night, doesn't it? Are you still jealous, after all these years?
Hélène I've got my whole family in that vault! My brother, my parents, my grandparents. You've only got your husband!

Marie What do you suggest for me, then? A pauper's grave?

Hélène Let me explain! I saw the person in charge of the vaults. Apparently they could dig an extension ... And then there'd be as much room as we wanted. But for that they'd have to remove those who are there already ... and then put them back again afterwards. (*Pause*) Horrible! (*Pause*) And there's something else. (*She looks for something in her bag*) It'd be very expensive. Even if we shared. He gave me an estimate. It'd cost about sixty thousand francs.

Marie Death gets dearer all the time.

Hélène (*with the estimate in her hand*) What do you think?

Marie (*after a pause*) If I were quite frank I'd say it didn't interest me in the least. But it's true there *is* a problem. Not for oneself, because one won't be there any more. But for those who are left, who have to find somewhere to bury you ... Places in vaults are expensive ... The most sensible thing would be cremation ... But that might be hard on the girls ... (*Pause*) Listen—how about this? If I die first, hard luck on you, I take the place. If you die first, I'll give in gracefully and find a quiet spot somewhere else. There must be some spaces left in the country, still, aren't there?

Sonia enters, puts the tart on the table and sits

Sonia I know of one that's perfectly charming ... Not so—select—but more poetic. A little cemetery not too far from Paris, just outside a village, among the fields. If you like I'll ask the price. I haven't got anywhere either ...

Marie We could lie there side by side—it'd be more cheerful!

Sonia (*laughing*) Tête-à-tête!

Marie (*laughing too*) In a huddle ...

Sonia Top to bottom?

Sonia bends down, grasps her ankles, and starts to walk about like this. Marie plays hopscotch. Hélène walks on all fours. They are all eight years old

Sonia		Kaiser Bill went up the hill
Hélène	(*singing together*)	To conquer all the nations
Marie		Kaiser Bill came down the hill
		And split his combinations.

Sonia (*to Marie, still with her hands round her ankles and her head down*) Marie! Can you do this?

Marie Like this? (*She imitates Sonia*) Oh no—*I* don't want to show my bottom. (*She starts to play hopscotch again*)

Sonia What shall we play?

Marie Yawning our heads off ...

Hélène (*to Sonia*) I'll be the lady in white and you be the soldier.

Sonia Ooh yes!

Sonia lies down and Hélène nurses her like a doll

Hélène My sweet little soldier—does his leg hurt, then?

Sonia No, it doesn't!

Hélène (*looking at Sonia's leg*) Oh, what a nasty leg! All black! Now who's going to cut the soldier's leg off?

She makes as if to saw Sonia's leg off. Sonia flees on all fours

Sonia (*yelling*) Help, help! I don't want to have my leg cut off!

Hélène (*running after her*) It's only in fun!

Marie circles round Sonia, holding up her thumb, round which she has tied her table-napkin

Marie Look at my baby! Hasn't she got a pretty dress?

Sonia (*quietening down*) A baby! Can I have a baby too?

Marie Spin round and round and you can have lots of them . . . ! Faster! Faster!

Sonia obediently twirls round with her eyes shut. Marie gives her a shove

Faster, faster!

Sonia falls over

Now *you*'re the baby!

Sonia You *are* beastly!

Hélène (*dancing round Sonia*) If you keep lying there they'll put you in a hole!

Marie A big black hole full of dust!

Sonia No they won't! They only do that when you're dead!

Hélène And when you're stupid.

Sonia gets up, crying, and hurls herself on Hélène

Sonia You're the one who's stupid! You're a stupid ass!

They fight. Marie tries to stop them

Marie Stop it! You'll hurt one another! (*Calling*) Madame! Madame! Hélène and Sonia are fighting!

Voice of Sonia's Mother (*with a strong Russian accent*) No quarrels, children! You don't stop you go home! I not tell again! You hear?

Hélène Yes, Madame.

Sonia and Marie make faces

Voice of Sonia's Mother You good now, Sonitchka . . . Little girls seen but not heard . . .

Sonia Yes, Mother.

Pause

Hélène (*to Marie, in a whisper*) Telltale tit! (*She pinches her*)

Marie Owww!

Sonia (*to Marie, also whispering*) Sneak! You're a sneak! (*She pulls her hair*)

Marie Owww! Oww! Madame, they're hurting me! Madame! Madame!

Marie runs out, crying and calling "Madame"

Hélène
Sonia } (*together; chasing her to the door*) Cry-baby! Water-works!

Marie is gone. The other two stand motionless, their backs to the audience.
Pause. There is a ring at the doorbell. Time has gone by and we are now at
another tea-party, a little later in the present. Nothing has changed

Sonia (*going to answer the door*) Coming, coming . . .

Sonia goes out

Marie (*to Sonia, off*) I tried to ring you but it was always engaged. It's just
like spring out.

Marie enters, carrying a small parcel and wearing her coat

Marie (*coming in*) Hallo. (*She kisses Hélène*) Am I late?
Hélène I just arrived.
Marie Laura dropped me off—she sends her love. (*To Sonia*) I brought
some raspberry macaroons—the kind you like . . .
Sonia You don't trust my Twelfth-Night cake!
Marie That's right!

Hélène sits down at the table. Marie takes off her coat

Hélène It looks delicious . . . Granny Suzanne's recipe?
Sonia Yes, but with fresh cream.
Hélène I must have a try at it one day. (*Looking round the table*) Of course,
there isn't any milk?
Sonia (*with a little shriek*) Oh, I completely forgot! You're the only person I
know who takes milk in her tea. Marie has lemon and I have jam. I'm so
sorry . . .
Hélène You have a convenient way of forgetting the very things——
Marie (*interrupting to change the subject*) I had some friends to dinner on
Tuesday. I gave them chicken tarragon. (*She sits on the chair on the right*)
Hélène Which friends?
Marie You don't know them. Friends of Jeanne's.
Pause
Hélène (*looking towards a corner of the room*) It looks as if you've been
tidying up at last.
Sonia Yes, I've done a bit of sorting out. To soothe my nerves. But what a
job! I wish I'd never started . . . It's so hard to know what to keep and
what to throw out. The complete works of Lenin, for example—would
they be worth anything?
Marie Maybe.
Hélène Do you mean to say you've got the complete works of Lenin?
Sonia They're André's. He left all his books behind when we got divorced
. . . he was so upset . . . (*To Marie*) I got out his stuff from the fifties for
you to have a look at. His "red" period.
Marie (*going over to look*) "Our" red period . . .
Sonia What a hoard, eh? He was a real hamster! I thought it would amuse
you. (*She sits on the chair on the left*)

Marie Up to a point. (*Taking down two or three pamphlets*) Kanapa, Jouvenel, Casa, Thorez—they're all here . . . The Soviet constitution, the most democratic in the world . . .

Hélène What's the point in dredging up all that nonsense? It's ancient history.

Marie Not for me. (*Reading*) "Let us answer the insults the lackeys of reaction hurl at Stalin by doing all we can to deserve the honourable name of Stalinist."

Hélène When I talked about dictatorship then, you and Jeannot wouldn't believe me.

Marie You were only giving the point of view of the Right.

Hélène I was saying what you say now!

Marie Yes, but now you almost make excuses for them!

Hélène And you're a fanatical anti-Russian. It's an obsession . . .

Marie I've become an anti-Stalinist! But you've always been anti-Communist.

Sonia (*to Marie, trying to smooth their differences*) We all thought we were doing the right thing, but we were mistaken, that's all . . .

Marie (*to Sonia, laughing*) Go on, fellow-traveller! I remember one morning at breakfast during the holidays, you tore open *The Communist Newsletter* and when we asked what you were looking for you said, "The results of the Russian elections"! In nineteen forty-nine! Even *we* laughed!

Sonia Well, it is my father's country—I felt concerned.

Marie (*reading*) "When my little boy looks at his portrait he calls him Grandpa Stalin. And it *is* a father's face that lights up our family table with a smile that radiates kindness and quiet strength."

Sonia and Marie roar with laughter

Hélène Stop fooling about! What's the matter with you both?

Sonia (*wiping her eyes on her napkin*) Oh my goodness—I cried nearly as much over Stalin's death as I did when my own father died . . .

Sonia and Marie go on laughing

Marie Yes, but you've never been a Communist . . . you've always been just a Russian—a petty-bourgeois nationalist!

They go on laughing

What did you do when you went to Russia for the first time?

Sonia (*putting on a strong Russian accent*) Knelt down and kissed sacred soil of ancestors . . .

Marie What was I saying? (*To Hélène*) Aren't you having any macaroons?

Hélène No thanks. I'd rather not risk it.

Sonia (*with her mouth full*) You don't know what you're missing! Mmm—they melt in your mouth!

Hélène Good . . . I had a terrible shock the other day. I was out somewhere, having tea, and I just took a bite out of a cake—not an especially hard one—and suddenly I felt my bridge break. These two teeth—here . . . (*She points to her two front teeth*)

Marie How awful!

Sonia Ouch!

Hélène I nearly swallowed my bridge with my cream slice! I rushed to the phone and rang Bernier, but I could scarcely utter. Had a job to make him understand. Fortunately he could take me right away!

Sonia You don't have to worry about my Twelfth-Night cake—it's as light as a feather . . . But watch out for the lucky charm!

Hélène When I think it might have happened in the holidays, away from Paris . . . (*Pause*) He asked me if I ground my teeth at night.

Marie I'm sure you do!

Marie and Sonia look at each other and smile. Pause. They all go on eating and drinking for a while

Sonia Did you listen to the debate yesterday evening on television?

Hélène Wasn't up to much, was it?

Sonia On the contrary! It was marvellous! I wouldn't have missed it for anything. You always learn such a lot . . .

Hélène What, for example?

Sonia (*taken aback for a moment, but then speaking with conviction*) That young professor who'd come over specially from America to tell us about his discoveries!

Hélène What exactly were they? I couldn't quite make out.

Sonia Neither could I. But he was so attractive!

Hélène A bit red in the face.

Sonia Oh, I thought it was my telly.

Marie (*taking the lucky charm out of her mouth*) I've got it!

Sonia (*standing up*) Three cheers for the queen! I'll fetch your crown.

Hélène (*to Marie*) You always get it.

Marie (*looking at it*) A star.

Sonia (*going out*) The star of the Three Wise Men.

Sonia disappears

Marie isn't listening. She's going back into the past

Marie "A six-pointed yellow star the size of a man's palm and outlined in black is to be worn on the left breast by every Jew over the age of six."

Hélène goes to fetch a man's nineteen thirties dress suit from the closet. We are back during the Occupation

Hélène Are you sure it doesn't fit your father any more?

Marie Absolutely. He bought it when he started out as a doctor, just after he was married. It's practically never been worn.

Hélène Marvellous material.

Marie English!

Hélène You wouldn't get anything like it now even on the black market . . . You ought to make yourself a suit out of it. Try it on. There's nothing to it. (*She hands the jacket and trousers to Marie*) All you need do is alter the shoulders, move the buttons, shorten the sleeves and take in the waist a

bit . . . And if you unpick the seams of the trousers you'll have enough for
a skirt. A straight skirt with a slit at the side.

Marie You don't think I'll look like a waiter with these silk lapels?

Hélène Not at all. You look very smart. You can be grateful to your father
for putting on weight.

Marie Hélène, I wanted to ask you something . . .

Sonia enters

Sonia By the way, did you know the fat ration's going down again?

Hélène Marie tells me you haven't collected your coal. It's crazy to miss
your coal ration!

Sonia I didn't miss it, it's just that the man I'm registered with hasn't got
any at the moment. I can change my lover but not my coal merchant!

Sonia exits

Marie (*to Hélène*) I wanted to ask you, could you take someone in for two
or three days? A friend.

Hélène Of course. Tell them to come at night. I'll be expecting them.

Marie Thank you.

Hélène Your father! Why did he go and register with the police? I've never
understood why he did it.

Marie You know what he's like. He fought in the last war, he's French, he
has the Military Medal and an identity card—what can happen to him?

Hélène Anything. Anything can happen to him . . .

Marie Jean has offered to get him false papers, but he refused. He doesn't
want to leave Paris . . . His apartment . . . his patients. (*She smiles*) Did
you know they come to see him in secret? He hasn't got the right to sign a
prescription now, but no-one can stop him making a diagnosis! (*Pause*)
He still has a surgery twice a week in a sports stadium out at Asnières, and
before he goes he fastens his coat collar over his star with press-studs!
(*She shows how with the dinner-jacket*)

Hélène That's dangerous!

Marie (*going and putting the suit away in the cupboard*) It's ridiculous. If they
find out he's a Jew . . .

Hélène Why did he go and register with the police?

Sonia enters suddenly

Sonia They've done it! It's just been announced on the BBC! The Russian
armies have joined up—the Germans are encircled!

They all embrace

Hélène At last! Thank God!

Sonia This time, my dears, they're done for!

Marie Stalin was right. There'll be dancing again in the streets of
Stalingrad.

Pause

Sonia What do you say to a little get-together for Twelfth Night, with a cake? Our little angels have an extra bit of sugar this month—we might as well make the most of it.

Hélène They really do spoil the younger generation!

Sonia Will Jean be able to come?

Marie Better not count on him for the moment. I'll contribute an egg.

Sonia Now all we need is some flour . . .

Sonia exits

Hélène Go on—you're perfectly capable of making a cake without flour!

Marie Sonia, the champion cook!

Pause. Marie puts her piece of cake in her mouth and eats it. We are back in the present at the second tea party

Sonia enters with a gold-paper crown

Sonia Hip hip hooray!

Marie (*enjoying the cake*) Terrific!

Sonia (*putting the crown on Marie's head*) I was afraid I'd used too much butter.

Marie (*solemnly*) It's the best you ever made.

Sonia Really? Would either of you like a little drink?

Hélène No thanks.

Marie You oughtn't to be drinking at this hour either.

Sonia (*going out*) Pardon me—it's after sunset. It's quite legitimate!

Sonia exits

Hélène (*rummaging in her bag; to Marie*) I've brought you a paper to sign. If you wouldn't mind casting an eye over it . . .

Marie What's it about?

Hélène The place in the vault.

Marie (*taking the paper*) You certainly stick to your guns!

Hélène I went back and saw Monsieur Roussel, the man in charge of the vaults. An amazing character! He talks about them as if they were apartments to let. With advantages and disadvantages. Some people like to be in the sun, others prefer the shade. High up, or in a hollow. Or near someone famous. On a main path or in a quiet by-way.

Pause

Marie And what about *my* body, *my* corpse, *my* mortal remains? What do you propose to do with them?

Hélène He says if you don't mind too much where it is you could easily find somewhere in the provinces.

Marie A sort of decentralization? (*Reading*) "It is hereby agreed between these present"—for the time being!—"that I the undersigned, Marie Rouvet, née Stern, of bla-bla-bla, waive all claims to the enjoyment"— that's a good one!—"of any rights in the plot granted in perpetuity to the above-named family and situate in the Allée des Platanes . . ." (*She goes on reading under her breath*)

Hélène Well? Do you agree?

Marie Hold on a minute. There's no hurry!

Hélène One of us might get run over by a bus.

Marie I wouldn't play you a trick like that! (*She puts the paper away in her bag*) I'd like to talk to the girls about it before I decide.

Hélène As you like.

Marie (*lowering her voice*) She doesn't seem to have heard about Grandpa Suliakov. And his shares.

Hélène Maître Tavel tried to ring her but she was always out. And his office has been closed over Christmas and the New Year ...

Marie It couldn't be a false alarm, could it?

Hélène Absolutely not, fifty thousand francs. Perhaps more. We spent quite a long time talking about it. He's going to suggest she invests it. Over five years. At a good rate of interest.

Sonia comes back with a bottle, a glass and a jug of water

Sonia Hot water for you two—vodka for me. (*She pours herself a drink*) Mmm ... that's the stuff!

Hélène (*after a glance at Marie*) Anything new on the financial front?

Sonia What could there be except new bloody problems? Ah well, thank goodness I've got the annuity ... that'll last me out! (*She chuckles*)

Marie Twelve hundred francs a month. It's not very much ...

Hélène What about your lump sum? Has it melted away?

Sonia (*vaguely*) Oh no.

Hélène How much have you got left?

Sonia I can't remember exactly ... But there must be something.

Hélène And what about your work?

Sonia I've never known exactly how much I earned—it's so irregular! When I still had some girls working for me I used to keep accounts, but now ... My old customers call in and look at my designs. Sometimes they buy something—it depends on the collections and what's in fashion.

Hélène But you must have some idea!

Sonia I manage. Giuliani dropped in this morning—my customer from Milan. He took some of the crocuses. Have I shown you my crocuses? Apparently prints are coming in again. Thank goodness for that! If everyone dressed in plain colours I'd be in the workhouse! Anyway, I'm on Social Security now—every little helps! (*She shows them her designs*)

Marie Crocuses! It's a lovely design. Lovely.

Pause

Hélène Has Victor given you back the two hundred francs he borrowed last month?

Sonia Did he borrow two hundred francs?

Hélène I had to lend you some money to last you to the end of the month!

Sonia I'll pay you back, don't worry.

Hélène (*eating*) You know perfectly well that's not the point. I just want to know how long you mean to go on letting yourself be fleeced.

Sonia It's not his fault if he can't find a job, poor boy! He does all he can. He looks.

Hélène He doesn't fall over himself!

Sonia If he'd had a bit of capital behind him to start with he'd have been able to buy some equipment and set up a lab. He could have specialized in photographs of racing cars—he's mad about cars! But what I earned from designing wouldn't stretch that far.

Hélène He could have done something else!

Marie That would have been a pity, with his talent!

Hélène Everyone's got talent. *His* chief talent seems to be for swinging the lead.

Sonia What's it got to do with you? Why don't you mind your own business?

Marie Yes, Hélène—you can't really understand their relationship.

Hélène Oh yes I can!

Marie You don't know what it's like to have children. You've said yourself you wouldn't have had children for anything.

Hélène That's true. And it gives me the horrors when I look at you two.

Sonia (*to Marie*) She's crazy! Mad!

Marie (*to Hélène*) What do you know about it? You've shielded yourself from everything. Nothing's ever touched you. You didn't need to work, you didn't marry, you've never had children. No-one's criticizing you— but don't go telling *us* what to do!

Hélène Oh, so you both think life is just work and husband and children? You both fell into line when you were twenty, and you've been in the same groove ever since! (*To Marie*) When did you start working?

Marie As soon as the girls were old enough.

Hélène You didn't need to. Jeannot was earning plenty, not to mention the family fortune.

Marie I wanted to work. I couldn't stay at home doing nothing. And I was interested in the art courses at the Louvre.

Hélène The work ethic! It's all right when you have to, like Sonia—but what's the point of working for working's sake?

Marie You don't mind spending your afternoons at the Sorbonne, listening to brilliant thinkers think for you.

Sonia (*to Hélène*) And five minutes ago you were criticizing Victor for not working!

Hélène That's different. He makes his mother work for him.

Sonia (*to Marie*) What's the point in arguing with her? It's like trying to explain jogging to a man with a wooden leg. (*To Hélène*) For one thing, Victor's very good to me. He comes to see me whenever he can!

Hélène Yes, to get money out of you.

Sonia He's so fond of his Hamilcar! (*To Marie*) She's been on the road since Sunday! We christened her in champagne. Titine, we call her. (*To Hélène*) And if I want to give him money it's *my* business. It's not your money— why must you interfere?

Hélène You're a lamb to the slaughter. As soon as he does you the honour of noticing you exist you start to purr.

Marie A lamb that purrs ...

Sonia Even if I gave him everything, I'd still be in his debt! (*Pause. As if to herself*) I was so fond of enjoying myself! I used to go out every evening. I told myself it didn't matter, because I loved him! And now I blame myself for not being a good mother ... for not showing him enough affection.

Pause

Marie That hotel, on the hill at Fiesole ...

Sonia And the pianist who played while we were having dinner ...

Marie No—the family *pension* ... with chairs outside and English newspapers. Victor made friends with a marvellous little girl with red hair.

Sonia No—Victor wasn't with us! He was in a summer camp in the Pyrenees!

Marie That was afterwards. You put him on the train in Rome.

Sonia Rome! I've never been to Rome!

Marie Of course you have! Victor didn't want to leave you.

Sonia Victor?

Marie and Hélène do not react to the following flashback scene

Victor enters from inside the apartment. He is a little boy

Victor Why can't I stay with you?

Sonia Because it's been settled you're to spend August in the mountains. It'll be good for you. The altitude, the fresh air—you look so pale.

Victor But I'd rather stay with you!

Sonia (*taking him on her knee*) Darling, be a good boy—don't make things difficult! It was so hard to get you in this year—there wasn't a single place left! I can't cancel now.

Victor But I never see you ...

Sonia Don't exaggerate! You see me all the time!

Victor But in Paris you always go out in the evening, and I have to have dinner all on my own—it's so boring.

Sonia I do the best I can! I have to work, you know!

Victor But you're on holiday now ...

Sonia Yes, but I need to relax ...

Short pause

You enjoy yourself in the mountains, don't you? You've got friends there?

Victor Yes—it's OK—but I'd rather be with you.

She kisses him

August will seem so long ... You will write to me, won't you?

Sonia Of course I will, darling! What will you be doing there?

Victor We're going to breed snails, me and some friend of mine. And we're going to build a log cabin. I do hope you'll write sometimes ...

Sonia Every day! Coloured postcards from everywhere we go!

Victor They say if we don't put on weight we get kept on longer. So I'm going to put on weight as fast as I can!

Sonia (*embracing him*) My little pink heffalump, my little blue clown, my honey bunny . . . Off with you now—(*she gives him a pat on the behind*)—go and pack!

Victor exits

We are back in the present

Hélène I have to hand it to you—two divorces and you're left without enough to live on! That takes some doing!

Sonia I suppose you think I should have claimed alimony? From Maurice? You must be out of your mind! It was as much as I could do to get him to pay anything for Victor! And he didn't even send that every month . . . (*Pause*) Men are funny. With them when it's over it's over. And even if you've had a child together they just forget it. Wash their hands of it! (*Pause*) A funny bloke, Maurice. Not very nice, really. The typical bright young Frenchman. A good thing he never took any interest in his son—he'd have ruined him! (*Pause*) I saw him the other day.

Marie No!

Hélène Maurice?

Sonia My first husband . . . He was going into a bar—I couldn't bring myself to call out to him.

Hélène Has he changed?

Sonia Yes. For the better. He's gone quite grey. Grey hair, grey eyes . . .

Marie Grey teeth.

They all laugh

Sonia It's funny. I was madly in love with him—I was quite ill when we parted . . . and yet now I can't even be bothered to say hallo to him. He doesn't exist for me any more.

Marie You cried your eyes out when you got divorced. I couldn't understand where you got all the tears from.

Hélène One day you were giving me the recipe for *tarte Tatin*—butter, caster sugar, sliced apples . . . And all the time your face was streaming with tears . . . They poured down your cheeks, and you went on talking, smiling, living . . . It was very strange!

Sonia (*thoughtfully*) Yes . . . but tears are only water . . .

Marie I liked your second divorce better!

Sonia My divorce from André?

Hélène (*smiling*) If you've forgotten your husbands you might at least remember your divorces!

Marie (*laughing*) Those insulting letters you wrote!

Sonia looks at her for a moment as if trying to remember, then suddenly gets up and paces about the room. They are all now fifty years old

Sonia (*exasperated*) Where the hell did I put them?

Marie (*getting up*) What?
Sonia (*on all fours by the bookshelves*) I was sure I'd kept the drafts!
Marie The drafts of what?
Sonia The injured party letters I wrote to Maurice for the divorce—I want to use them again for André.
Marie (*sitting down in the armchair*) You don't think they might have dated a bit? It'd be better to write some new ones.
Sonia OK. (*She sits on the floor and gets hold of a piece of paper*) "My dear André . . ."
Marie That doesn't sound very injured. Just put "André".
Sonia (*writing*) "André." He's quite a good bloke really . . .
Marie (*laughing*) That's enough! "André . . . I've had enough of your continual bad temper . . ."
Sonia (*writing*) Poor thing—he's always laughing! Always good-humoured. It gets on your nerves. You wake up thinking everything's hopeless, all is vanity—and there in front of you is that cheerful mug—I could punch him right on the nose!

They all laugh

Marie ". . . and I'm fed up with your always being away . . ."
Sonia (*writing*) He's a real stay-at-home—the trouble I had to winkle him out.
Marie ". . . and the blatant way you flaunt your infidelities . . ."
Sonia (*throwing down her pen*) No—I can't!
Marie Why not?
Sonia Because it isn't true!
Marie But he's agreed to play along and accept all the responsibility! We have to say something!
Sonia But it isn't nice . . .
Marie Who cares? No-one's going to read these letters. (*Pause*) You *are* sure you want a divorce?
Sonia Oh yes! I adore André but he bores me to death . . . How on earth did I manage to live with him for fifteen years? I think it was because of Victor—they got on so well together . . . But now Victor's left home I can get divorced!
Marie André was a real father to him.
Sonia (*tenderly*) I told him he had to take the calf with the cow . . . And he was so sweet . . . The day Victor had his appendix out he brought him every comic he could find! The hospital bed was covered with them. For a kid of twelve it was heaven!
Hélène (*getting up suddenly*) Don't you two find it hot in here?
Marie Would you like me to open the window?
Hélène That wouldn't help . . . I feel hot inside. It's as if my face, my whole head, were flooded with hot blood . . . and then suddenly I go quite cold! It's horrible!
Sonia It happens to all of us . . . It's only Nature.
Hélène And I suppose Nature's always right? What about typhoons, and earthquakes, and epidemics? If Nature says women's lives have to stop at

fifty, Nature's got it wrong. I refuse to accept Nature.

Marie It's not life that stops—it's the power to give life.

Hélène But I never wanted to give life! I couldn't care less about that. What I can't stand are these fits of anxiety, this chaos, this feeling that everything is draining away. This minor death. (*Pause*) Don't you two feel anything?

Marie No. But don't worry—it'll come.

Sonia With me it's just the opposite. When I think how little time I have left I feel like doing all sorts of crazy things ... They do you so much good! (*She smiles, and lies down like an odalisque*)

Pause

Marie You ... !

Sonia How did you guess?

Marie It's not difficult. When you start looking like a cat that's swallowed the canary.

Sonia (*after a short pause*) I met him in the street ...

Hélène What do you mean—"in the street"?

Sonia A man—coming out of the cinema. He came up and spoke to me.

Hélène And you went with him?

Sonia He invited me for a coffee. He seemed so pleasant and polite I didn't like to refuse.

Hélène You're quite mad! At your age?

Sonia That's just it. I thought: "What have I got to lose? Men don't abduct women of fifty. Unfortunately." (*She laughs*)

Marie And?

Sonia We walked for a bit—over by Menilmontant ... it's so pretty round there ... We talked about this and that, and then suddenly he stopped and said he wanted me.

Marie And?

Sonia (*after a pause; smiling*) It was very nice. I'd always wanted to make love with a stranger. (*She gets up*) It's very agreeable. Nothing left afterwards but the pleasure.

Hélène (*coming back to the table*) He might have been a sadist—a criminal—a pervert!

Sonia (*also coming back to the table*) I was lucky. He was very gentle.

Marie (*following the other two*) Have you seen him since?

Sonia Oh no—that would have spoiled everything ... ! I came home. I had an appointment with André. For dinner. I found him even more boring than usual.

They all sit, smiling. We are back in the present. Sonia eats a macaroon and heaves a deep sigh

Never again. Never again will someone come up to me in the street. Want me. The way men used to look at me as they passed ... The question— "Yes or no?" (*Pause*) I was quite right to enjoy it while I could. (*She pours herself a drink*) As Juliette Vigne used to say: "The last train's gone, kiddos!" (*Pause*) I gather she's dead.

Hélène Who?
Sonia Juliette Vigne. Cerebral haemorrhage.
Hélène I hadn't heard. Was it recently?
Sonia About two years ago.
Hélène How old would she be now?
Sonia Oh ... the same age as us ... give or take six months or so ... she'd
be sixty.
Hélène Everyone's dying now!
Marie Juliette Vigne?
Hélène The daughter of the lady downstairs, at home!
Marie Juliette Vigne ... I do seem to remember something ...
Sonia We were in the same class for two years!
Hélène A tall dark girl with a perm!
Sonia And she'd had her ears pierced!
Hélène And she used mascara!
Sonia And powder!

Hélène runs to the window. They are all fifteen

Hélène Come and look! Hurry up!
Marie We're coming!
Hélène (*her nose pressed to the window*) Juliette Vigne's got a new boyfriend!
Sonia (*rushing over*) What's he like?
Hélène Too late, my dear—they've gone into the tobacconist's.
Marie (*scandalized*) You don't mean to say she's started smoking too?
Sonia She doesn't care what she does!
Hélène He'd got his arm around her waist ... like this ... (*She puts her arm
round Marie's waist*)
Sonia I suppose you saw there was a man waiting for her when we came out
of school yesterday?
Marie How old?
Sonia At least twenty-five!
Marie Perhaps it was her brother?
Sonia Her Siamese twin! They were absolutely glued to one another!

They all burst out laughing

Hélène She was letting someone kiss her in the porch the other day, in the
dark. What a slut!
Sonia How could you see if it was in the dark?
Hélène I heard! She was letting out little gasps: "Mmmm ... Mmmm ..."
Marie There they are!
Sonia He's not bad-looking ...
Marie I don't like his moustache.
Sonia I bet it tickles!
Hélène (*to Marie*) Stop shoving!
Sonia Do you know what she told me?
Marie No—but we're going to.

They all laugh

. . .

Sonia (*lowering her voice*) She told me she never wore knickers . . .
Hélène How disgusting!
Marie She must feel cold in the winter . . .
Sonia (*laughing*) That's why she snuggles up to men—to keep warm!
Hélène (*vehemently*) I'll never take my knickers off—not even to go to bed!
Marie So how will you ever have children?
Hélène I don't want any. I want to stay with my father and mother and brother. And no-one else.
Marie Not even us?
Hélène No. Just the four of us.
Marie Silly ass!

Hélène turns away. Marie and Sonia go on looking out of the window

Jean (*off*) Hélène! (*Pause*) Hélène!

Jean enters

Hélène . . . come here . . .

Hélène goes over to him, reluctantly

What's the matter? Why are you so sulky? What have I done? (*He tilts her chin*) Tell me!
Hélène (*after a pause; almost inaudible*) You don't love me any more!
Jean What?
Hélène No . . . you don't talk to me any more . . .
Jean But I'm talking to you now! Aren't I?
Hélène (*obstinately*) Not like before. Before, it was always just the two of us. We didn't need to talk . . . It was just us . . .
Jean (*gentle exasperation*) What do you want, exactly? Do you want us to talk or not?
Hélène I want you to love me . . .
Jean But I do love you!
Hélène I want you to love only me . . .

She doesn't look at him. He takes her by the shoulders

Jean Listen, sweetie. I love Marie, and I don't see why I should hide it from you any longer. But I love you too. You're my little sister.
Hélène (*tearing herself away*) Get away from me! I'm not asking you any favours! You've been had! You've let yourself be hooked! You don't belong here any more—get out! I was a fool to love you so! You didn't even suggest the three of us could live together! Now it's all over . . . I hope you drop dead . . . I hope you all drop dead!
Jean I hope *you* know you're completely mad! What do you want?
Hélène (*obstinately*) I want you to stay here with us! I don't want you ever to leave us!
Jean (*gently*) But I still love you just as much as I always have. Marie doesn't stop me loving you. (*Pause. Not very convincingly*) We can all three live together if you like. It'd be wonderful!

Hélène Clear out!

Jean leaves

Hélène remains downstage with her back to the audience. All three come back and sit down, talking as they do so. We are in the present

Sonia No, what bothers me is not so much dying as the thought of being buried lying on my back, with my feet all that distance away ...

Marie They could hardly tie them round your neck!

Sonia I'd like to be buried curled up, like when I'm in bed ... I've never slept on my back, and I don't want to start in my coffin!

Hélène You absolutely have to make yourself conspicuous!

Marie She's not the only one! Neanderthal man was buried in the foetal position!

Sonia (*to Hélène*) Obviously to make *him*self conspicuous!

They all laugh

Marie (*to Hélène*) What she needs is a jar to be buried in.

Hélène (*to Marie*) Can you see Victor looking for a jar?

Marie And standing upright, like Clemenceau!

Hélène Or flat on her face, like adulteresses in Ethiopia!

Marie Talking of which, what's become of old André?

Sonia Didn't I tell you? He's getting married to one of his students!

Hélène }
Marie } (*together*) No!

Sonia Thirty years younger than he is! He's taken to wearing check suits. Thinks it makes him look younger, I suppose. He looks like Grock!

They laugh

Hélène When he was forty he used to wear houndstooth. Now it's checks. He'll end up in a horse-blanket.

Marie I thought his experience with you had cured him of marriage.

Sonia He *did* stay single for ten years!

There is a ring at the doorbell. They all look at each other

Who can that be?

Hélène Don't go. I know a woman who was forced to ... strip naked ... in her own apartment ...

Sonia My dream!

Hélène Yes, but afterwards he held her at knife-point for three hours. She only escaped by a miracle!

Sonia Still naked?

Another ring at the door

Hell, I'm going. (*To Marie*) If I get killed you can have my kimono.

Sonia goes out

Hélène (*going towards the door*) Why don't you get a spy-hole put in?

Marie (*getting up*) Ask who it is before you open the door!

*Hélène and Marie stand upstage with their backs to the audience. Long pause.
A clock strikes five. A week has gone by, the third tea party has begun. Hélène
paces to and fro. She looks at her watch*

Hélène She must have forgotten! She forgets everything! She's got a
memory like a sieve.

Marie No, she hasn't forgotten. I spoke to her on the phone this morning.
She had to go out for something first thing this afternoon. She must have
been held up. (*She takes a book from the bookshelves and sits in the
armchair. She looks tired*)

Hélène She isn't looking well lately, is she?

Marie She's worried about Victor.

Hélène What's he done now?

Marie That's just the point! Nothing!

Hélène Couldn't she forget *him* for a bit?

Marie (*reading*) You can forget your lungs, but you can't stop breathing.

Hélène Of course. Sorry. I forgot. Flesh of your flesh, and all that. (*Pause*)
I've always thought women overdid their so-called special relationship
with their children. Men have money, power, work . . . Women have to
have something! So they've invented the maternal instinct. "You can't
explain it—you have to have experienced it."

*Marie has fallen asleep. The book drops from her hand. Hélène turns and looks
at her. Pause. The phone rings. Nearly forty years ago*

(*As if about to answer*) Yes . . .

The phone rings again

(*As if she were answering it*) Yes. . . . No, he's not here—he's just gone out.
. . . I've no idea. He only called in to change—he hadn't slept all night. . . .
No, I'm his sister . . . What? . . . When? . . . But they said nothing would
happen before this evening! . . . A boy, I hope? . . . Oh well, we'll get used
to the idea. . . . Yes, I'll be right over.

*Hélène comes and kneels by Marie, who is now sleeping as if with her baby in
her arms*

(*Softly*) Marie . . . Marie . . . it's me.

Marie (*waking*) Look . . . a little girl . . . When I opened my eyes the doctor
was holding her upside down. All shiny. A little silver fish.

Hélène moves aside

Jean comes in, goes and bends over Marie

Jean (*softly*) What's it to be, then—Hermine or Jeanne?

Marie Jeanne.

Jean She looks like a wrinkly old Chinaman . . . When I got here just now I
went straight to the delivery room, where I'd left you . . . there was a
woman on the operating table with her nightdress turned back and her
hands on her stomach. She was screaming, with her mouth wide open.
When I went in she turned her face towards me . . .

Marie And?

Jean For a moment I thought pain had made you unrecognizable. And then suddenly I realized it wasn't you. That they'd taken you back to your room. That you'd been, as they put it, "delivered".

Marie Jean, I feel low. Why?

Jean You're tired.

Marie No, it's not that. (*Pause*) I'm not the youngest any more. I'm in between. Mortal ... (*She shuts her eyes*)

Jean kisses her and goes out

Pause. We are back to the present

Hélène I didn't want to have children. I got my wish all right. (*Pause*) The fourteenth of July, nineteen thirty-six ... My boyfriend was a medical student. He'd said, "If there's any blood, take out the probe and call me." We got a taxi and went to a not too fussy nursing home out near Joinville ... I felt as if all my blood were draining out of me ...We drove through suburbs full of people dancing and singing ... fairy lights ... fireworks ... And there was I, afraid I was going to die in the taxi!

Pause. Marie wakes and picks up the book she dropped earlier

A funny thing—I always managed to have my abortions on days of national importance. May the eighth, nineteen forty-five. VE Day. All France was out in the street, and I was in bed with a probe in my uterus ...

Pause

Sonia (*off*) Anyone in? Hélène? Marie? Are you there?

Sonia bustles in, breathless but cheerful. She is carrying parcels

Hallo! I'm so sorry—I had to wait half an hour for a bus. The traffic! (*She kisses them*)

Hélène We were afraid you'd forgotten about us. We *did* say half-past four, didn't we?

Sonia Forgotten you! I left the key in case ... You *did* find it? (*She puts down her parcels*) I met Victor in the street. On his way to see his mamotchka. I asked him along to taste my cherry tart. You don't mind, do you?

Marie You must be joking.

Victor enters

Victor And here he is! And are all my godmothers dying to give their dear little Victor a kiss? (*He kisses Hélène*)

Hélène We can just about contain ourselves ...

Marie And how is Master Flibbertigibbet?

Victor (*kissing her*) In cracking form.

Marie I forgot your birthday on Monday—very sorry!

Victor You were quite right! Forty—what a thought! If I get run over on my way home the papers will describe me as middle-aged. Imagine! (*He sits*)

Sonia (*taking her coat off*) We're so excited! Guess what the concierge had waiting for me? You'll never guess! A letter with "Maître Tavel, lawyer" on the envelope! (*To Hélène*) What are you looking like that for?

Hélène (*with a peculiar expression*) I'm not looking like anything. I'm waiting to hear.

Sonia (*turning the letter over and over*) What *can* it be?

Hélène Open it and you'll see!

Victor No, wait. Make it last. Let's pretend first. Suppose it was some money!

Sonia (*gazing at the letter*) Money?

Victor Yes . . . You could buy anything you want . . . Just like when you won five thousand francs in the lottery!

Sonia (*to the other two*) That was on the twenty-fourth of December, nineteen forty-six! The only time in my life I ever got anything for nothing . . .

Victor helps himself to a biscuit from the table and starts to nibble at it. We are in the past and Victor is a child

(*Going over to him*) Vishya, my angel – have you been a good boy?

Victor Yes, Mother.

Sonia Did you do the shopping?

Victor Yes, Mother. I got some ham, and some grated cheese for the noodles. And some yoghurt. And some chocolate for me.

Sonia Did the grocer say anything?

Victor Yes. He wanted to know when you'd be back . . . I'd told him you were away so he wouldn't bother me about the bill! He brings it up every time . . .

Sonia Poor Vishya! But that's all over now – he won't bother you any more. Darling – what was it you asked for for Christmas?

Victor An electric train. A real one, that works! With an engine, and sleeping coaches, and a restaurant car, and everything!

Sonia Look in your play-box.

Victor (*looking at his play-box, then at Sonia*) What is it?

Sonia Look and see.

Victor goes over to the box

Open it!

Victor opens the box and takes out the engine

Isn't it a lovely engine? There's an orange one for the goods train. (*She takes out the rails*) You can arrange the rails however you like – in a circle, or an oval, or a figure-of-eight . . .

Victor Where *is* the goods train?

Sonia Here. (*Setting out the rails*) It's got three trucks. With tanks.

Victor Can I make it go straight away!

Sonia No problem. Just put the engine on the rails . . .

He does so

Then we connect it up . . . (*She attaches the rails to the transformer*) And plug it in . . . (*She does so*) And switch on . . . (*She does so*) And off it goes!

The engine doesn't move

But what's the matter!

Pause. They look at each other

Victor Perhaps it's broken?
Sonia (*suddenly hitting herself on the forehead, realizing what's wrong*) Oh hell and damnation!

Victor and Sonia burst out laughing and embrace. We are back in the present

Victor (*to the other two*) She'd forgotten the electricity had been cut off!
Sonia And as it was Christmas it was two days before I could pay the bill and be reconnected!
Victor Right. Now let's be serious and see what's in the letter.
Sonia (*opening it and reading*) "Dear Madam: Would you kindly call in at my office as soon as possible in connection with a matter concerning you. Yours faithfully, Maître Tavel."

Victor and Sonia exchange glances

Victor Maybe there was still a little bit due to you?
Sonia No, I don't think so . . . Papa inherited quite a lot of money, but when he died it was all we could do to scrape up enough to bury him. I never could understand what became of it all. Maybe he had a lady-friend? Or gambled at roulette? Anyhow, we were left penniless overnight!
Victor So what can it be?

Pause. They go on looking at each other

Why don't you phone and find out?
Sonia Brilliant idea!

Sonia goes out

Victor eats. Pause

Hélène You seem to be fond of cherry tart.
Victor I'm fond of everything.

Pause

Hélène Are you working just now?
Victor (*his mouth full*) Oh, just odds and ends . . . But if our situation should improve (*pointing to the envelope lying on the table*) I'll be able to make my dream come true at last.
Hélène What dream's that?
Victor Doing a real job on Titine.
Sonia (*off*) Engaged!
Marie But your little Hamilcar is fine as it is!
Victor Yes, but she'd be even better with a six-cylinder engine . . . (*To*

Sonia) Remember that accident I told you about at Arpajon, Mother—
the C Six? Well, I absolutely must find that Englishman ...
Sonia (*off*) You could make inquiries at the hospital.
Victor (*getting up*) That's it! They'll have kept a record of the driver's
address even if he's kicked the bucket. His pals mentioned that he lived in
Somerset ...

Sonia returns

Maybe we could drive down and buy what's left of the car ... Then Pierre
could come with the trailer——
Sonia —and we could drive back across country——
Victor —and I could do a feature to cover part of the expenses ...
Sonia But that's not the point at the moment.

Sonia goes out again

Victor You can make the most marvellous finds! When I think of the
treasures buried in those auto graveyards ... rusting and mouldering
away for years. (*He sits*) All the sparking plugs ... and the radiators ...
and the valves ... and the carburettors ... (*Cutting himself a piece of tart*)
Instead of wasting their time excavating the tombs of Rameses or
Tutankhamun! Do you realize all those fantastic things are still there?
Cam-shafts that are real antiques, rocker arms that haven't been seen
since the days of de Dion and Bugatti, helical gears as peerless as the
Venus de Milo! Doesn't it make you dizzy!
Hélène Intoxicated!

Sonia returns

Sonia Engaged all the time ...
Victor (*standing up*) Would you like me to go and see him? (*Consulting his
watch*) With a bit of luck I'll get there before the office shuts, and I'll ring
you right away. OK?
Sonia All right.
Hélène All this sudden activity!
Victor (*to Sonia*) Could you slip me a few francs? Titine's in dock and I
think I'll take a taxi to save time ...
Sonia (*rummaging in her bag*) I've only got a hundred-franc note ...
Victor (*taking it*) I'll call in with the change ... Right, I'm off! *Ciao,*
Godmothers!

Victor goes out, followed by Sonia

Sonia (*off*) You didn't tell me what happened about the photos ...
Victor (*off*) They didn't have room for them this month ... But they've
promised to put them in next ...
Hélène He'll make short work of those shares!
Marie (*smiling*) He's just a child. A great big child of forty!
Hélène An elderly little boy. Did you notice how he eats? Guzzles, rather ...
Marie That's just to reassure himself.
Hélène (*looking at the empty plates*) I wouldn't have minded reassuring
myself a bit!

Marie His need is greater than yours.
Hélène How do you know?
Marie It's too late for you now. And for me. (*She smiles*) Roger and out.
Hélène Very droll!
Marie (*flicking through the book, which she's still holding*) Not really.
Hélène Always making jokes ... Gets on one's nerves ...
Marie It mightn't do you any harm if you tried to understand them.
Hélène Do you mind not talking to me as if I were mentally deficient?

Their middle-aged squabble becomes a childish one, and their whole behaviour changes. Hélène is doing her homework and Marie is memorizing something under her breath. The book has become a collection of recitations. They are twelve years old

Marie Idiot! (*She goes on reciting under her breath*)
Hélène You're as flat as a pancake!
Marie It's this blouse ... I'm as developed as you are, really!
Hélène Jeannot called you a little brat.

Sonia comes in during the following

Marie Fat lot I care—I can't stand him! (*Pause*) I thought I was going to die during the night ... I couldn't breathe ... I called Mother, and she was so frightened she started to cry!
Sonia And then what?
Marie She called the doctor. He said it was my nerves.

The other two stare at her in amazement. She isn't sorry to be in the limelight

They're sending me to the mountains.
Sonia What about school?
Marie They said that didn't matter—I needed rest.
Sonia You *are* lucky!
Marie (*self-importantly*) You wouldn't think so if you were me. You don't know what it's like to gasp for breath ... I wish I didn't, I can tell you!
Hélène (*counter-attacking*) The doctor said I ought to have showers to help me sleep!
Marie Yes, but you don't gasp for breath!
Hélène And some tablets with a difficult name—it ends in "xine"—two tablets every night ...
Marie I take tablets too—in the morning, at midday *and* at night!
Hélène And all since the day a man followed me on the stairs ... and showed me his what-d'you-call-it ...
Sonia What did you do?
Hélène I was so frightened I couldn't move. And he wanted me to touch it.
Marie Oh my goodness!
Hélène And I didn't know how to explain it to Mother. So I said "Mother, the gentleman showed me his willy."
Sonia What did she say?
Hélène And for a week afterwards I had plain-clothes policemen with me all the time so that if I met him again I could point him out to them ...

Marie I always have the same nightmare . . . My grandmother has died. I'm walking down a long corridor with a doorway at the end. And on a couch by the telephone is my grandmother . . . She's dropped the phone, and been sick all over the place. It's very dark. And I'm afraid she's not quite dead!

Sonia (*to get her share of the limelight*) When I grow up I'm going to do ballet!

Marie Bally what?

Hélène and Marie laugh

Hélène Do you mean you're going to be a ballet dancer?

Sonia Mademoiselle Petrovna said I was gifted!

Hélène Oh do show!

Marie Oh—yes please, Sonia!

Sonia does a few steps, humming a few bars of vaguely classical music. The other two imitate her behind her back, then end up in peals of laughter

Hélène Do you know what everyone calls you at school?

Sonia (*stopping in the fifth position*) No?

Hélène Sack of potatoes!

Marie Fat-face! Fat-face Sonia!

They roll about laughing

Sonia (*to Hélène*) Well, you've got piggy eyes!

Hélène Do you want a kick up the backside?

Sonia And do you want a punch on the nose?

Marie It was only a joke!

Hélène Fat bottom!

Sonia Right on the snout?

Voice of Sonia's Mother (*Russian accent*) Aren't you ashamed of yourselves, big girls like you? Stop it at once!

Hélène and **Marie** Yes, Madame.

Voice of Sonia's Mother Dushka—you're good now, aren't you?

Sonia Yes, Mother.

As they quarrel they've come back round the table, sitting down to answer Sonia's Mother's voice. Marie in the middle, Hélène to the left, Sonia to the right. Pause. They are back in the present

Marie (*wistfully*) Fat-face Sonia . . .

Sonia (*looking at herself, sighing*) I lost a lot of weight afterwards. A shadow of my former self. Seven kilos less of Sonia. But they tied up my tubes after I had Victor, and I went up like a balloon. Like with neutered cats. And to think I had such a fine bosom! Well, I've certainly worn *that* out! (*Pause. She fingers the lawyer's letter*) I hope it's not more trouble. (*Pause*) I hope he gets there before they close! What time is it?

Hélène He'll get there soon enough!

Sonia Oh yes, of course—for you there's no hurry! You have no imagination whatsoever when it comes to other people.

Hélène Do you mean to say *you* take any interest in anything but your precious son?

Sonia I remember one day ... I'd just come out of hospital after my gallstone operation ... I didn't have a single franc. And you started to lecture me about how wasteful it was to order coal fifty kilos at a time. "Why don't you buy it by the ton?" you said, with all the assurance that comes from having plenty of money. "Much more practical!", you said.

Hélène And so it would have been!

Sonia You didn't once stop to ask yourself if I could afford to pay for a ton! A detail beneath your notice.

Hélène You only had to ask me for the money!

Sonia No! It was for you to ask me if I'd accept it ... You ought to be more polite than other people when you're rich.

Hélène So that they'll overlook it? It isn't a venereal disease, you know!

Sonia No, but it doesn't give you the right to judge other people, either! Don't think I don't notice your condescending tone: "How can you bear to live in such a place? I couldn't stick it for three days!"

Hélène But it could be charming if you had done it up!

Sonia What if I can't afford to?

Hélène It's not a question of money!

Marie It never *is* with people who've got plenty! But just the same, the sin against the Holy Ghost is to treat their precious money lightly.

Hélène Why do you have to stick *your* oar in?

Sonia She's quite right. Things have to be said ...

Hélène Especially if they're unpleasant!

Sonia Marie didn't mean to hurt you!

Hélène No—Marie never means to hurt ... Marie is outspoken ...

Marie Yes, I am.

Hélène Marie has to tell the truth.

Marie I think it's the simplest way, all things considered.

Hélène For *you*! The simplest way for *you*!

Marie For other people too.

Hélène Not necessarily.

Marie What are you referring to?

Hélène When Jeannot was ill ...

Marie Well?

Hélène Telling him.

Marie Are you afraid to say the word? We'd promised one another that if either of us had cancer we wouldn't lie about it. I kept my promise.

Hélène You forced him to make a superhuman effort. Instead of making the little time he had left a bit easier.

Marie But it was you who tired him out, with your hysterics and your blind faith in the first quack who came along! (*Pause*) I never told him he was going to die. I said he had cancer. And that we'd do all we could to save him. And that he must fight too. (*Pause*) You can't treat the man you love like a feeble-minded child.

Pause

Hélène But you and your doctors couldn't cure him! Any more than my quacks could!

Jean enters and stands motionless in the hallway, watching them

Marie No. But we were together through it all. (*Pause*) I even helped him to die. You didn't know that. When there was no hope left. When it had spread to the brain. (*Pause*) "Marie—help me." That was the last thing I heard him say. And then communications were cut off. Just one word, over and over: "No ... no ... no ..." (*Pause*) He started to suffer. So I gave him a slightly stronger dose of morphine and he went to sleep. My three years as a medical student came in useful for that at least.

Pause

Hélène Have you ever told the girls?
Marie (*to Hélène*) No. It was a private matter between him and me. (*Facing the audience*) Isn't that right, Jean?
Jean Yes, Marie—that's right.
Marie Where are you now.
Jean Nowhere. When you call to me, it's you yourself who answer.
Marie You were losing your hair.
Jean Yes.
Marie You'd put on weight ...
Jean (*smiling*) I was always saying I'd go to gym classes ...
Marie You worked too hard ...
Jean I was always saying I'd take a break and we'd travel ...
Marie Later on ...
Jean You complained that I neglected you. You were jealous.
Marie Forgive me. (*Pause*) You know, Jean—I'm not the same person you used to know. If you passed me in the street you wouldn't recognize me!
Jean Nor you me!
Marie And if I stopped thinking about you?
Jean Then I'd cease to exist. Even the dead can die!
Marie (*to herself*) There's no-one who really knows me any more ...
Hélène Marie, would you like some more tea?
Marie Yes, please ...

Jean goes

Sonia cuts herself a piece of tart and starts to eat it off the knife

Sonia—for goodness' sake! Not off the knife! You'll cut your mouth.
Hélène You look like an old peasant munching cheese in a field!
Sonia (*pleased*) That's the moujik in me! My roots! (*She chuckles*) Do you realize, my pets—if it hadn't been for Stolypin and Red Sunday in St Petersburg I wouldn't be here eating cherry tart with you? It's delicious, by the way! I'd have been born somewhere in the Ukraine ...
Marie And have died somewhere in Siberia.
Sonia Not necessarily ... You've got to die of something whether it's Stalinism or bronchial pneumonia. (*Pause*) I had a phone call last night.

From my cousin Suliakov—the one who's a physicist near Novosibirsk. She wanted me to send her some scientific magazine. There was a funny noise on the line. I asked her if she could hear it. She said, "Yes—it's the wind!" Imagine that! I heard the wind blowing in Siberia ... here in this apartment.

Hélène looks in her compact and repairs her lipstick. Marie and Sonia collect up the plates and cutlery

Hélène What a sight! It's hardly worth bothering. (*She lifts the skin on her face*) Once you're middle-aged you have too much skin, and that's a fact!

Pause

Sonia (*going to fetch a tray*) The older I look now the better I like it!

Marie gets up

Marie Can I help with the washing up?
Sonia What—just three cups and saucers? I'll do them with my plate after dinner.

They stack the plates and cutlery and tea-pot on the tray

Hélène Is Madame Marcelle still ill then?
Sonia Yes, poor woman!
Hélène It's you who's the poor woman!
Sonia Oh, there's not much housework when you live on your own.
Marie Nor cooking. I never get to sit down any more for meals. I just have a piece of cheese standing up, watching the news.

Marie takes the tray out to the kitchen

Pause

Sonia (*to Hélène*) That reminds me ... I was meaning to ask you ... Do you think you could lend me five hundred francs? I'll let you have it back at the beginning of next month without fail! (*Pause*) I'm a bit overdrawn at the bank.
Hélène Since when?
Sonia Oh, two or three days ... They're usually very nice and don't make too much fuss, but there's a new manager who's a bit of a stickler ...
Hélène What went wrong?
Sonia The electricity bill was more than I expected, and as it's debited straight from my account ... They really are the limit—they don't come and read the meter for six months and then they sting you for two thousand francs all at once!
Hélène What about the famous lump sum? I thought you said there was still some left?

They put the sugar-bowl, the jam and the napkins away in the cupboard. Only the three tea-cups and the glass of vodka are left on the table. They put the chairs back to where they were at the beginning of the play

Sonia (*babbling*) Yes ... But I had some ... I had to buy some ... stuff ... paper ... various things ... It's only for a few days ... I'm expecting some ...

Hélène Don't take me for a fool, please. If you need money, it's obviously for Victor!

Sonia (*feebly, picking up her glass*) It's not for Victor, it's for me, for the electricity ...

Hélène It's for you because you haven't got a bean left; because you've given him all you had; because if you had millions you'd give him the lot; because it'll always be the same! What a mess! Listen, Sonia. If your son won't work that's his funeral. If you want to keep him, you have a perfect right to do so. If you like being fleeced, that's your business. But what's it got to do with me? He's not my son, I have no duty towards him, he doesn't interest me in the slightest, I don't give a damn about him! I've had enough of being the mug, the sucker ... It's always *your* problems ... what about me? Have you ever thought about me? I could be struck down on the spot and you wouldn't even notice ... so long as your greedy old kid could go on playing with his toy cars! (*She sits, with her back to the audience*)

Marie enters and stands looking at her

Sonia I'm fed up! Fed up! I've never been so fed up! The more I think of it the more fed up I am ... (*She sits in the armchair*)

Hélène You'd feel better if you stopped drinking.

Sonia You remind me of the girl at school who always used to say I had ugly hands.

Hélène It was me.

Pause

Marie (*to Hélène*) You haven't asked me what I've decided about the vault.

Hélène I was just going to.

Marie We've talked it over, the girls and I.

Hélène And?

Marie It's not easy.

Hélène But what did you decide?

Marie There are two alternatives: either I stand on my rights, or I withdraw ... (*Pause*) If I stand on my rights there's only one solution: dig a bigger hole. A bit gruesome, I agree, but once it's done there'll be plenty of room—we could even invite a few friends ... (*Pause*) It'd cost sixty thousand francs. Thirty thousand each.

Hélène That's right.

Pause

Marie Right. Now we come to the second possibility: I let you have the place.

Hélène That would be very kind.

Marie Yes. And you'd save thirty thousand! Correct?

Hélène Yes.

Marie Well now. After much deliberation we arrived at the following conclusion—unanimously—Laura, Jeanne and myself. You keep the place, but you pay compensation. Key money, if you like—twenty thousand francs. Your eternal rest should be worth that much. (*Pause*) You save ten thousand. And you stay with the family.

Hélène Very well. I'll send you the cheque tomorrow.

Marie Make it out to Sonia.

Sonia Me?

Hélène But why?

Marie It seemed to us that was the only thing to do with the money. (*Pause. She sits*) We couldn't quite reconcile ourselves to where it came from, if you see what I mean? And at least with Sonia we can be sure it won't last long!

Sonia (*merely seeing she has got out of a scrape*) Just like a fairy tale ...

Pause

Hélène (*facing the audience again*) It seems quite ridiculous to me. But just as you like.

Pause. They are all sitting down. Far away from one another. During the following, they talk either to themselves or to Jean

Jean enters and stands listening to them upstage

The women all face the audience

Marie (*to Jean*) That was the best solution, wasn't it?

Hélène (*to Jean*) They're always against me. I'm all alone.

Sonia (*to Jean*) Did you see how nasty she is? Always on about my Victor ... (*Pause*) She hasn't been laid enough, that's her trouble—a case of all-round frustration. And the chaps she used to pick for herself! Poor thing ... They were always either married or cracked or dim—sometimes all three! The textbooks call it a failure complex. (*Pause. To Jean*) She'd have done better to sleep with you ... Skol! (*She raises her glass and drinks*)

Hélène How can you stop being afraid? Of everything that crawls or hides or springs out at you from everywhere. Of noises at night ... I put a chair up against the door, but with my earplugs I wouldn't hear anything anyway ... And what about the windows? I can't put bars up everywhere, can I? It isn't difficult to break a window—and I could scream till I was blue in the face ...

Marie Every evening I go to bed later, but it doesn't help. (*Pause*) I lie on the right side of the bed. I've kept your side for you ... your bedside table ... your lamp. (*With a little laugh*) But I borrow your pillow for reading. (*Pause*) First something to make me sleep. As little as possible. I make resolutions that don't convince even me ...: "Just one tonight ..." I keep the barbiturates for special occasions. When I decide to give myself a little treat. Falling asleep like a stone. Into the void. Nothingness. Heaven.

Sonia Not making love any more ... I don't miss it all that much. (*Pause.*

To Jean) One day you asked me to sleep with you. It was in the summer. Marie was in Brittany with the children. You went on about how wonderful it would be. You said I had a bedroom voice. (*Pause*) Why do you men always have to talk so much? I didn't feel like it.

Hélène I've given up going to the country. Here at least there's the neighbours. (*Pause*) But at night the streets are deserted. Not that I go out any more. I don't have the television too loud so as to hear if anyone tries to get in. I leave the key in the lock and bolt the door . . .

Marie I choose the biggest and dullest book I can find . . . A treatise on monetary reform or an article on the fertility of marriages in the south-west quarter of France between seventeen twenty and eighteen twenty-nine . . . (*With a little laugh*) That's how I come to have so many odd bits of knowledge. I cling on to every line, every sentence, every word. I only switch the light off when I can't keep my eyes open any more.

Sonia (*to Jean*) You men always thought I was a floozy because of the way I behaved. I liked to be liked. I needed to be liked. (*Pause*) Where is she now, the little Sonia of my palmy days? When I used to go to school in evening dress after being up all night dancing? I tucked my skirt up under my overall and went to sleep on my desk. The teacher used to say, "I hope I'm not disturbing you?" and I used to say, "No, not at all!" and go back to sleep again . . . (*Pause*) And the arts ball! (*She hums a tune of the period*)

Hélène What if I'm taken ill in the night, all on my own? And haven't the strength to phone? I could peg out and no-one would notice! And how would they get in, with all those bolts . . . ? (*Pause. To Jean*) You used to leave the door open between our rooms. So I could call you, you said, if the erl-king came to carry me off . . . "*Wer reitet so spät durch Nacht und Wind?—Es ist der Vater mit seinem Kind . . .*"

Marie And every night, in the dark, it's always the same.

Jean goes

I start tossing and turning and going over and over everything in my mind—things I didn't do, things I ought to have done, things it's too late for. I recast my life in every possible way, but it always ends in tatters . . . (*Pause*) The wisdom of the old—don't make me laugh! If age could . . .

Long pause. The clock strikes once. Marie looks at her watch

Do you know what time it is? Half-past six! I must go! (*To Hélène*) Will you drop me?

Hélène Of course.

Sonia Going already? Do stay a bit longer! What's the hurry?

Marie I have to collect a coat from the cleaner's for Laura. They close at seven.

Hélène and Marie go to fetch their coats from the adjoining room

Sonia Go tomorrow instead. I've got tons of things to tell you . . . We never have time to talk . . .

Hélène (*off*) Tell us next Thursday!
Sonia Are you really going then? What a shame!

Hélène comes back

Hélène (*kissing Sonia goodbye*) I bet I've got a parking ticket already!
Sonia Oh no!—they never come round this way! See you next week, then!

Hélène goes. Marie comes back in her coat

Marie Phone me as soon as you hear what Tavel was on about.
Sonia Of course! (*She kisses Marie goodbye*) So long as Victor's in charge . . .
Marie (*smiling*) Yes . . . See you next Thursday then!

Marie and Sonia go out

(*Off*) Thanks for the cherry tart!
Sonia (*off*) Thanks for the twenty thousand!
Hélène (*off*) You should be thanking *me*!
Sonia (*off*) See you Thursday!
Hélène (*off*) See you Thursday!
Marie (*off*) See you Thursday!

Pause

Sonia comes back, leaving the door ajar

She wanders round the room for a while, then sits down on the divan. After a while we hear a voice with a Russian accent, the voice we've heard before from the next room

Voice of Sonia's Mother Maïa devotchka, rest now, be quiet . . . Dushka, dushenka . . . Lie down now, and go to sleep.

Pause. Sonia lies down

Little girls should be seen and not heard. (*Pause*) Lie still. Don't talk. I'll turn off the light so you can go to sleep.

Pause. The Lights go out in sequence, as though Sonia's mother is switching them off, leaving only a low glow upstage as if from a light in the next room

Don't be frightened, Sonitchka . . . I'll leave the door open.

Sonia gives a little whimper

Don't cry—there's a light in the next room. Shut your eyes . . . Sweet dreams!

Pause

The CURTAIN *slowly falls*

Good-night now, dushenka!

FURNITURE AND PROPERTY LIST

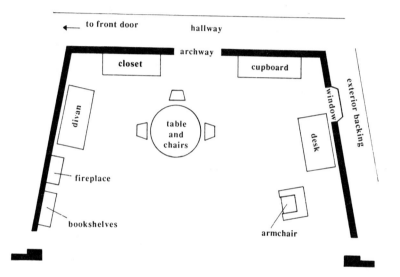

On stage: Divan. *On it:* cushions, cover

Table. *On it:* artificial flowers, wig in a box, powder compact, eyebrow pencil, lipstick, hairpins

3 chairs. *On one:* kimono

Cupboard. *In it:* glasses, small plates, cups, saucers, bottle of wine, box of biscuits, sugar-bowl and tongs, tea-cosy and mat, tablecloth, napkins, cutlery

Closet. *In it:* 1930's man's dress suit, work-basket containing needle, thread and scissors

Desk. *On it:* clutter of papers, including designs for fabrics etc., pens, pencils, desk-lamp with light bulb. *Beside it:* play-box containing electric train set

Armchair

Fireplace. *Above it:* mirror. *Beside it:* books, pamphlets, papers, pens, etc. on shelves

Off stage: Radiator cap in a package **(Victor)**
Package **(Hélène)**
Tray containing pot of tea, dish of lemon slices, pot of jam **(Sonia)**
Plate of tart with knife **(Sonia)**
Small parcel containing raspberry macaroons **(Marie)**
Gold-paper crown **(Sonia)**
Bottle of vodka, glass, jug of water **(Sonia)**
Parcels, unopened letter, handbag containing 100-franc note **(Sonia)**

Personal: **Victor:** doorkey, button, wristwatch
Marie: handbag, lucky charm, wristwatch
Hélène: wristwatch, handbag containing compact with mirror, lipstick, estimate, paper, pen

LIGHTING PLOT

Practical fittings required: table lamps. Interior. The same scene throughout

To open: General lighting

Cue 1   Pause. They are all sitting down   (Page 40)
           Dim lighting very slightly

Cue 2   **Voice of Sonia's Mother:** "... can go to sleep."   (Page 42)
           Pause, then snap off practicals in sequence, leaving dim light
           upstage as if from a light in the next room

EFFECTS PLOT

MADE AND PRINTED IN GREAT BRITAIN BY
LATIMER TREND & COMPANY LTD PLYMOUTH

MADE IN ENGLAND